LIVE
YOUTH

CW01433347

Second
Chance

Iris Howden

Published in association with
The Basic Skills Agency

Hodder & Stoughton
A MEMBER OF THE HODDER HEADLINE GROUP

Cataloguing in Publication Data is available from the British Library.

ISBN 0 340 696931

First published 1997
Impression number   10 9 8 7 6 5 4 3 2 1
Year   2002 2001 2000 1999 1998 1997

Typeset by Fakenham Photosetting Ltd, Fakenham, Norfolk.
Printed in Great Britain for Hodder & Stoughton Educational, a division of Hodder Headline Plc, 338 Euston Road, London NW1 3BH by Athenaeum Press Ltd, Gateshead, Tyne & Wear.

Second Chance

Contents

1	The Crash	1
2	Sadness	6
3	Learning	13
4	Aunt Peg	19
5	New Life	25
6	Jamie	30
7	Christmas	36
8	Moving On	40

1

The Crash

I don't remember the car crash.
I woke up in a hospital bed.
My head hurt a lot. I could not move.
Wires coming from my arm
were linked up to a drip.
Then I heard my mum's voice.
It sounded a long way off.
'Nurse! Sally's awake. Thank God.'

They told me later I had been in a coma
– asleep for ten days.
The crash had been head-on.

My boyfriend, Rob, who was driving,
was lucky. He was thrown from the car.
He landed on soft grass at the edge of the road.
My side of the car
took the full force of the crash.
I had steel pins put in my legs
to hold the bones together.
My right arm was broken.
Five ribs were cracked.

I was in hospital for weeks.
From there I went to a special home
at the seaside, called Green Gates.
It was a place for people like me,
who had been badly hurt in accidents.

My spine was damaged in the crash.
At first I didn't know that.
I thought that I would get better.
That I would soon be up and about.
My arm mended, my ribs healed.
The cuts and bruises on my body faded.

It seemed only a matter of time
before things got back to normal.

Mum came down at weekends to see me.
It was hard on her. She had a good job.
Mum needed to work.
She had brought me up on her own
since my dad died when I was small.
I was proud of her.
She always looked so smart,
so young for her age.
She never let things get her down.
It was a shock to see her in tears one Saturday.

She was late. I sat by my bed for ages,
thinking she was in a traffic jam.
Then I saw her come into the ward,
wiping her eyes. She looked very tired.
Mum gave me a kiss and turned away.
She began to unpack her bag
and put things away in my locker:
clean nightdresses, some sweets and magazines.
I knew she was crying.

'What's the matter, mum?' I asked.
She turned to face me with tears in her eyes.
Mum always told the truth.
She had never kept secrets from me.
It was the same now. She said the doctors
thought that I would never walk again.
I would be in a wheelchair
for the rest of my life.

I didn't know what to say. At first
I felt more sorry for mum than for myself.
She looked so upset.
Later, when she'd gone home,
I sat alone, thinking about what it meant
never to walk again.
The nurse came in with my supper.
I couldn't eat a thing.
She asked me if I wanted to watch TV.
I shook my head. I didn't want to talk.
I turned my face to the wall,
wanting to cry. But the tears wouldn't come.
I didn't feel anything at all.
I just felt numb.

We were kept busy at the home each day
so I didn't have time to think much.
We had time with the physio staff,
learning all the skills we would need
to cope with life in a wheelchair.
I began to build up the strength in my arms.
Soon I could pull myself in and out
of my chair.
I could dress myself and so on.

People told me I was lucky.
My brain wasn't harmed by the accident.
My face wasn't scarred.
But I didn't feel lucky. I felt like a freak.
My life would never be the same again.

The weeks passed.
I could get around quite well in my chair.
'You'll be coming home soon,' mum told me.
'We'll have a party for you.
A welcome home and a birthday party in one.'
I had forgotten about my birthday.
I would be seventeen in a few weeks' time.

2

Sadness

Back home, my friends from college
were on holiday for the summer.
I thought about them, out swimming,
playing tennis, having a good time.
I used to love sport.
Rob and I liked walking, skating,
riding our bikes together.
Now I couldn't bear to think of him.
He'd sent flowers to the hospital,
written to me while I was at Green Gates.
But he hadn't come to visit me – not once.

'It's been hard for Rob as well,' my mum said.
'His car is all smashed up.
He blames himself for the accident.
Things will be different when you get home.
Wait and see. He'll be round all the time.'

Mum was full of plans for the party.
I went along with it, sat in the garden
and made a list of people to invite.
I had asked all my old friends
and quite a few people from Green Gates.
They were coming in a minibus.
I began to look forward to it.

When the day came I was nervous.
Mum had had things fixed for my chair.
There was a ramp at the front door,
a handrail in the bathroom downstairs.
My new bedroom was right next door.
The wallpaper and curtains were pretty.
It all looked fresh and nice
but it felt strange. I longed to go
upstairs to my old room but I couldn't.

My mum had asked a hairdresser to come in
to do my hair.
She helped me into my new dress.
Then we drove to the hotel
she had booked for the party.
The food was laid out on a long table.
There were vases of flowers all along it.
A big cake iced in pink and silver stood at one
end. HAPPY BIRTHDAY SALLY
it said on the top.
There were seventeen candles round it.

'All this must have cost the earth,' I said.
'It's worth every penny,' mum told me.
'I want you to enjoy your birthday.'
She looked lovely in her black silk dress.
You could always rely on my mum
to put on a good show.

At one end of the room there was a dance floor.
A man was setting up a music centre.

'I didn't know there would be a disco,' I said.
'Oh, yes,' my mum replied.
'People will expect it.'
My friends from college began to arrive.
They all brought presents. Soon there was
quite a pile beside my chair.
They told me all the news.
Who had passed their exams.
Who had got a job.
Who was going out with someone new.

The room began to fill up.
I looked round, hoping to see Rob.
It was quite late when he came in.
His sister, Val was with him,
and another girl I didn't know.
'I hope you don't mind,' he said quietly.
'Val brought her French penfriend.
She's staying with us for a month.'
'Of course not,' I told Rob,
pleased to see him at last.
The French girl's name was Martine.
She was very pretty with long black hair.

The crowd from Green Gates had all come.
They sat in a circle watching the dancing.
Rob hung about for a while, not saying much.
He looked bored. We didn't seem to have
anything to say to each other.
'Go and have a dance with Martine,'
I told him.
'If you're sure?' he said, leaving quickly.
I moved my wheelchair to join
my disabled friends.
Suddenly I felt more at ease with them.

Some of my friends from Green Gates joined in
with the music. They sang along to it.
Waved their arms in time to the beat.
I couldn't do that. I'd have felt silly.
I hated having to sit there watching
while my college friends danced.
I wanted to be up there with them.
Rob and Martine moved well together.
He kept his arm round her
when the record stopped.
I wanted him to hold me not her.

Martine looked up at him and laughed.
I knew then it was all over between us.

Mum came up with her boss, Mr Davis.
He had dropped in to bring me a present.
It was a bottle of perfume.
'Happy Birthday, Sally,' he said.
'Sweet seventeen, eh?
This is a good party your mum's put on.'
I tried hard to smile. To look as if I meant it.
'Yes,' I said. 'It's great.'
The party went on till midnight.
I hated every minute of it.

Back home, I went straight to bed,
telling mum I felt tired.
Lying there in the dark, I began to cry
for the first time since the accident.
Tears rolled down my cheeks
as if they would never stop.
I wished my life had ended in that crash.
I wished I was dead.

3

Learning

After the party I went through a bad patch.
My mum was out at work all day.
A woman came in every morning to clean up
and make my lunch. She was very fussy
and would not let me do anything for myself.
She even put sugar in my tea and stirred it.
I suppose she felt sorry for me.
Mum said I could ring Julie,
her friend next door,
if I needed anything in the afternoon.
But I never did. I got used to being alone.

At first my friends called round.
They never stayed long. I had nothing
to tell them. I began to feel sorry for myself.
Sometimes I didn't bother to get dressed.
It was easier to sit in my dressing gown
and watch TV all day.

My mum was worried. She tried to talk to me.
To make plans for the future.
'You can't go on like this,' she said.
'You should go back to college.
Repeat your first year. Learn to type.
You're a bright girl.
You'd soon get a job in an office.'
'I don't want a job in a stupid office!'
I shouted. 'I wanted to teach sport!
Well, that's out now I'm stuck in this chair,
isn't it? I could rot for all anybody cares!'

Mum didn't say anything.
She went into the kitchen to make supper.
I could hear her banging
the pots and pans about.

When she came back her eyes were red.
I knew she had been crying but I couldn't
bring myself to say I was sorry.

The next day she brought home a big box.
Inside was a home computer.
It had its own printer and everything.
Mum gave me the handbook and left me to it.
'I'll never get the hang of this,'
I told her crossly. 'It's too hard.'
'Rubbish,' mum said. 'Read the book again.
By the way, there's a teacher coming in
tomorrow. It's time you caught up
with your college work.'

The teacher's name was Bill.
He was quite young.
He had a beard and he wasn't bad looking.
We went over the work in my file.
'You're lucky to have a computer,' he said,
'I wish I could afford one like this.'
Bill helped me set up the printer.
'Make a start by typing up your notes,' he said.

'You'll soon catch up if you try.'
I learned to type quite well.

When Bill came next he was pleased.
'Well done, you're making progress.'
Bill was a good teacher.
He never lost his temper.
He made the lessons seem fun.
I asked my mum if he could come more often.
'Of course,' she said.

She never minded paying
for extra things I wanted.
So Bill came twice a week.
Sometimes I would ask him to stay a bit
longer. To explain something
or have a game of scrabble.
I would think of ways of keeping him there.
I liked his company.

One day he was late.
I thought he wasn't coming.
After about an hour he turned up.
'Where have you been?' I asked.
I wanted to get started.
'My car broke down.' He sounded cross.
He looked hot and sticky.
His hands were black with oil.
'Why don't you get a new one?' I asked.
Bill's car was a real old banger.
'What would I use for money?' he said.
'We're not all spoilt brats.
I haven't got a mummy to buy me
anything I want.'

He tried to make it seem like a joke
but I knew he meant it.

Bill made up the time we'd lost.
When the lesson ended
he picked up his briefcase.
'Aren't you going to stay for a game of
scrabble?' I asked.
He shook his head. 'I must get home,' he said.
'My mum will pay for an extra hour,'
I told him.
'I have to baby-sit tonight,' he said.
'My wife's going out.'
He stopped and looked at me in a strange way.
'You know Sally,' he said.
'One day you'll find out
that money can't buy everything.'

4

Aunt Peg

At the end of the summer
my Aunt Peg came to stay.
She was my father's sister.
She came every year.
We were the only family she had.
Aunt Peg ran a market garden up north.
She could never stay long because of that.

She was a big, plump woman
who always looked untidy.
None of her clothes went together.
Mum made jokes about them and said that Peg

bought her outfits from a jumble sale.
But I thought she was nice.
She was kind to me and she always
brought a present.
One year it was the scrabble set.
This time she gave me a huge round jigsaw.
It had over two thousand pieces.
'That should keep you busy,' she said.

In some ways Aunt Peg was quite strict.
When I was little I always had to
mind my manners.
She hadn't changed.
On Monday when my mum went off to work
she made me peel the potatoes.
'Make yourself useful, girl,' she said,
dumping the bowl in my lap.
Mum was pleased when she got home.
'That was kind of you, Sally,' she said.
I didn't say anything but I felt a bit mean
about all the times I had left her to peel the
potatoes after a hard day's work.

One day mum came home looking happy.
She and Aunt Peg were talking in the hall.
They stopped when they saw me.
'Go and put the kettle on, please, Sally,'
Aunt Peg said.
'Your mum could do with a nice cup of tea.'
She shut the door behind me,
so I couldn't hear what they were saying.
'Why should I make the tea?' I thought.
'They can get around better than I can.'
But I did it all the same.

I knew Aunt Peg thought I was lazy at times.

The next day Aunt Peg and I were sitting
in the garden. It was a lovely day.
'You should get out more,' Aunt Peg said.
'You look pale. Why stay indoors all day?'
Then she told me my mum's news.
Her boss, Mr Davis, wanted her to go
with him to America.
They would be working in New York
for six weeks.
'But she can't!' I said. 'What about me?'

Aunt Peg looked at me hard.
'What about you?' she said.
'It's your mum we're talking about.
This is a big chance for her.
She's worked for years to give you
everything you want.
It's time Joyce thought of herself for once.
I've told her she must go.'

I didn't say anything but I was cross

that Mum had told Aunt Peg her news first.
That Peg told her to go.
'But what about me?'
'What would happen to me?'
I knew even as I spoke that I sounded
Like a spoilt little child.

'You could go back to Green Gates for a
while.' Aunt Peg said.
'Or you could stay with me.'
'In Yorkshire?' I said.
I had never been to visit Aunt Peg.
'Why not?' she said. 'It would be a change for
you. You've got to start leading
your own life some time.
And letting your Mum lead hers.
Joyce is still young.
She's a good looking woman.
She might want to marry again.'

I felt my face go red.
Mum had gone out with one or two men
over the years. One of them, Ben

had wanted to marry her.
He was really quite nice and I knew
she had turned him down because of me.
I made it clear I didn't want a stepfather.
I wanted my mother all to myself.

I thought about that now,
turning things over in my mind.
Bill had called me a spoilt brat.
Aunt Peg thought I was lazy and selfish.
I didn't like myself very much at that moment.
So I made up my mind to make it up to mum.
I would tell her to go to America
while I went to stay with Aunt Peg.

5

New Life

It was dark when we got to Aunt Peg's village.
We drove through quiet streets
then down a narrow lane to the house.
I heard a dog bark inside.
Then a young man came out
to open the gates.
'Who's that?' I asked.
I thought Aunt Peg lived alone.
'That's Jamie,' she replied.
'I couldn't manage without him.
I rang him and told him to get a room
ready for you downstairs.'

Jamie nodded to me.
He began to unpack the car,
taking in first my bags,
then the computer from the back seat.
He looked about twenty or twenty-one.
He had dark, curly hair.
His clothes were scruffy. His jeans were torn
and there was a hole in his jumper.

The house wasn't any better.
Books and papers lay about on the chairs.
The sideboard was piled high with boxes.
But the room looked cosy.
There was a bright fire burning in the grate.
'I've cooked a meal,' Jamie told Aunt Peg.
He didn't say a word to me.

Soon we were sitting at the big old table
eating stew. We drank tea out of mugs.
I thought about the meals we had at home.
Our table set with pretty china and a cloth.
Here everything seemed so rough and ready.

There wasn't pudding, just cheese and hunks
of bread. I had to admit it tasted good.

Next morning when I woke up,
I drew back the curtains.
Outside was the most lovely view
I had ever seen.
There were hills and fields on all sides.
The sun was shining. It was a beautiful day.
I dressed and went through to the kitchen.
There was no sign of anyone. Empty plates
had been left on the table. I found a packet
of cornflakes and some milk and helped myself.
The clock on the wall said ten to nine.

Aunt Peg was outside, in the greenhouse,
putting little plants into pots.
Jamie was digging away in the next field.
Aunt Peg passed me a tray of plants and some
pots. She handed me a tiny fork and trowel.
'Put a bit of that soil in the bottom of each
pot, she said. 'Ease the plant out gently.
Put it in the pot and pack some soil round it.

Then firm it in with your fingers, like this.'

I did my best but it was a tricky job.
I looked at the few I had done,
then at the rows of pots Aunt Peg had filled.
'I'm not very good at this,' I said.
'You'll soon pick it up,' she said.
She sorted out some big plants
that looked dead.
Their leaves were dry and brown.
'Are you going to throw those away?' I asked.
'Bless you, no,' she said.
'Everything deserves a second chance.'
She cut each one down
and put a plastic bag over it.
'Some of these will grow again,' she said.
'They'll be as good as new.'

6

Jamie

The days passed quickly.
I helped with the plants every morning.
Then I would get a simple meal ready
for our lunch; soup and a sandwich
or bacon and eggs.
In the afternoons I worked at my computer.
I could listen out for the phone
and take messages for Aunt Peg.

After tea we sat by the fire.
Sometimes we read or put the radio on.
Aunt Peg didn't have a TV set.

I thought it would be boring but it wasn't.
It was peaceful with the dog and the cat
asleep on the rug.
Aunt Peg often nodded off too.

Jamie was nice when I got to know him.
I think he was just shy.
We often had a game of cards
or else we played scrabble.
One night, after the game, he wrote
a message using the letter tiles.
D O Y O U W A N T T O G O
O U T?
So I put – W H E R E T O?
He added the words T O T H E P U B.
I put O K. It made me laugh.
It seemed a daft thing to do
but I guess Jamie found it an easy way
to ask me to go out with him.

We went to the Red Lion pub in the village.
The bar was small and cosy.

Jamie got a shandy for me and a half pint
of beer for himself.
We sat and watched some men playing darts.
I began to enjoy myself.
It made a change to go out.
I liked the way Jamie treated me.
He didn't act as though I was different.
Of course he hadn't known me before
the accident. Maybe that helped.
Anyway, we soon became good friends.

After that he often took me out.
I went with him in the van to deliver plants.
It was autumn. The trees were at their best.
Their leaves were turning red and gold.
I came to love the countryside around us.
And I grew very fond of Jamie.

One day I asked him how he had come to
know Aunt Peg.
'It's a long story,' he said.
'Are you sure you want to hear it?'
'Go ahead,' I told him.

'Well,' he said. 'When I was younger
I was always in trouble.
My mum and dad split up when I was a kid.
Mum got a new man and I hated him.
I moved out when I was sixteen.
I lived in a hostel. Then on the streets.
Soon I was robbing to get money for food.
I broke into your Aunt's house one night.
She came downstairs and found me in the
kitchen. Only she didn't ring the police.

She sat me down and talked to me.
I found myself telling her all about
the way I had been living.
Anyway, your Aunt took me in.
She said everyone should have
a second chance.
Peg's been great to me. I owe her a lot.
She gave me a home and a job.
She even sent me to college.
I did a botany course to learn about plants.'

'You've been to college?' I asked.
Jamie gave me a funny look.
'You're not the only one with an education,'
he said. 'I may not look very smart.
You get dirty working on the land, you know.'
'I'm sorry,' I said. 'I didn't mean ...'
Sometimes I wished I could keep my big
mouth shut.
Jamie laughed. 'I'm only teasing you,' he said.
'You take everything to heart.
What about you? What are your plans?'

I told Jamie about the car crash.
About Green Gates and the birthday party.
About losing Rob. Even about Bill
calling me a spoilt brat.
'I didn't know about the accident,' Jamie said.
'I thought you had always been in a
wheelchair. You seem to cope so well.'
I felt very pleased until he said.
'Anyway, I don't think you're a spoilt brat.
A bit stuck-up maybe ... only joking,' he said
seeing the look on my face.
'You manage really well.'

'I wish I could do more to help,' I told him.
'You and Aunt Peg work all hours.'
'Hang on,' Jamie said. 'Can you type?
Do letters, that sort of thing?'
I nodded. 'Why?' I asked.
He went to the sideboard and took down a box.
It was stuffed with letters and bills.
'These need sorting out,' he told me.
'Aunt Peg and I never seem to get round
to the paperwork.'

7

Christmas

After that I spent most of my day
sorting through the papers.
Aunt Peg told me what to say and I wrote
answers to all the letters.
I sent out bills and made a start
on the accounts.
'I wish I knew more about this,' I said.
'Maybe I could take a bookkeeping course
when I go back to college.'
'Oh, so you do plan to go back to college,'
Aunt Peg said. 'Your Mum seemed to think
you weren't too sure about that.'

'I may as well,' I told her.
I was beginning to enjoy office work,
now I could see some point to it.
Later, when we had played scrabble,
Jamie put down one of his messages.
WHEN DO YOU GO
HOME? it said.
I put the answer SOON and felt sad.
I WILL MISS YOU
was his reply.
I'll miss you too, I thought.

Then Mum rang from New York.
She said that Mr Davis wanted to stay on
for a bit longer. They might not be home
until after Christmas.
She asked me how I felt about that.
'I don't mind at all,' I said,
which was the truth.

We had a wonderful Christmas.
We were busy right up till the last minute.
Lots of people came to collect pot plants.

They came to buy their Christmas trees.
The phone never stopped ringing.
I bought Jamie a warm checked shirt.
I got a record for Aunt Peg.

We didn't make a big fuss.
We had a turkey for dinner, of course,
with a bottle of wine.
Then we had the mince pies I had made
and some fruit and nuts.
I thought back to the Christmas Days at home,
where we always had a huge tree,
a cake, some crackers, all the trimmings.
My mum bought me masses of presents.
I looked at the book Jamie had given me.
The warm rug over my knees that was
Aunt Peg's present to me.
I had everything I wanted here.
I had not been so happy for a long time.

Before we began our game of scrabble
Jamie laid out a special message
with the tiles. I LOVE YOU, it said.

In the warm light from the fire,
with his new shirt on and his hair combed
for once, he looked really good.
I added one word to make it say:
I LOVE YOU TOO.
Jamie found the X and pointed to it.
I knew what he meant and laughed.
Aunt Peg was beginning to doze off.
Behind her back we stole our first kiss.

39

8

Moving On

My mum came back for the New Year.
I was pleased to see her, of course.
But I didn't want to go home.
I didn't know how to tell Mum that.
I waited till she was out.
Then I spoke to Aunt Peg.
I asked her if I could stay on.
To my surprise she said no.

'Why not?' I said. 'I thought you liked
having me here.
I've tried to make myself useful.

Who's going to do the paper work?
Answer the phone?'
'You've done very well,' Aunt Peg said.
'And I love having you here. But you'd be
even more use if you went to college.
You could take bookkeeping and so on.
Then you could come back and work for me.'

'There's Jamie,' I said. 'We'll miss each other.'
'Of course you will,' she said, 'but it will be
a good test for you. Find out how you feel
after a few months apart.
Besides,' she said, 'you owe it to yourself.
To face up to the real world again.'
'What do you mean?' I asked.

'When you came here you were hurt and angry,'
Aunt Peg said. 'You wanted to hit back
at everyone. I've watched you grow up.
You've come to terms with
being in a wheelchair.
Now you have to find out what life has to offer.
It's nice and safe, tucked away up here.

Nobody asks too much of you.
I'd like to see you go back to college.
Mix with people again. Get some skills.
Take your exams. You should learn to drive.
Then you could get yourself about,
and choose where you want to be.
You know I love you, Sally.
But I'd be selfish to keep you here now.'
I leaned forward and kissed her cheek.
I knew in my heart that she was right.
'Thanks for everything,' I said.

My mum came in, her arms full of parcels.
'Come on Sally,' she said. 'Help me get ready
to see in the New Year.'
Some of Aunt Peg's friends from the village
were coming round for a drink.
It turned into quite a party.
Jamie and I did not have a chance to talk.
I still had not told him I was going.

At last, we were able to talk.
He held my hand and looked into my eyes.

But I did not have to tell him. He knew.
'You're going back aren't you?' he said.
'Yes,' I said. 'I think it's for the best.'
I told him what Aunt Peg had said.
'It makes sense when you think about it.
I'd be a lot more use if I could do
the office work really well,' I said.
'I know,' he said. 'This is your second chance.
And you've got to take it.'

I heard the sound of bells. It was midnight.
Another year was about to begin.
We joined arms and sang 'Auld Lang Syne.'
Then Aunt Peg clapped her hands.
'Quiet, please,' she said. 'I want you all
to drink a toast. To Sally.
To a new start at college in the new year.
'To Sally,' they said. 'A Happy New Year.'
My eyes met Jamie's across the room.

Later, when all the guests had gone,
Jamie went out to check the greenhouses.
I found the scrabble set on the sideboard.

We had forgotten to pack it.
I made up my mind to leave it there,
ready for when I came again.
I set up the board where Jamie would see it
next morning, after I'd gone.
I moved the little white tiles around,
to leave a final message.
One I meant with all my heart.

WAIT FOR ME I put.
TILL I COME BACK